CHARLES B. & PATRICIA A.

TUBBS
CHILDREN'S
LIBRARY

Animal Behavior

Animals Building Homes

by Wendy Perkins

Capstone press

Mankato, Minnesota

First Facts is published by Capstone Press,
151 Good Counsel Drive, P.O. Box 669, Mankato, Minnesota 56002.
www.capstonepress.com

Library of Congress Cataloging-in-Publication Data
Perkins, Wendy.
   Animals building homes / by Wendy Perkins.
   p. cm.—(First facts: Animal behavior)
   Summary: Simple text explains the varied ways in which such animals as beavers,
hummingbirds, termites, and bald eagles build their homes.
   Includes bibliographical references (p. 23) and index.
   ISBN 0-7368-2509-6 (hardcover)
   ISBN 0-7368-5161-5 (paperback)
   1. Animals—Habitations—Juvenile literature. [1. Animals—Habitations.] I. Title. II. Series:
First facts. Animal behavior.
   QL756.P475 2004
   591.56′4—dc22   2003015213

Editorial Credits
Erika L. Shores, editor; Jennifer Bergstrom, series designer; Wanda Winch, photo researcher;
   Eric Kudalis, product planning editor

Photo Credits
Bert Katzung, 19
Bruce Coleman Inc./Bill Wood, 13; Charles Summers Jr., 20; Daniel Zupanc, 12; Jeff Foott, 7; 14–15
Corbis/D. Robert & Lorri Franz, 17
Dwight R. Kuhn, 9
Erwin and Peggy Bauer, cover, 10–11
Minden Pictures/Konrad Wothe, 8
Tom & Pat Leeson, 5

**First Facts thanks Bernd Heinrich, Ph.D., Department of Biology, University of
Vermont in Burlington, Vermont, for reviewing this book.**

1 2 3 4 5 6 09 08 07 06 05 04

Table of Contents

A Beaver's Home

A beaver is hard at work. It gnaws on a tree trunk. Soon, the tree falls. The beaver floats the log to a pond. There, the beaver builds a **lodge**. The beaver piles up logs. It fills the cracks between the logs with mud and grass. The lodge keeps the beaver safe and warm.

Safe at Home

Most animals need a home. Homes keep animals safe from **predators**, rain, snow, or the hot sun. Some animals live in their homes for life. Other animals live in their homes long enough to raise their **offspring** or **survive** hot or cold weather.

 Fun Fact:
Foxes have more than one home. Foxes move their young to a new home if a predator comes near.

Building Nests

Many animals live in nests. A hummingbird builds a small cup-shaped nest. The nest is made of moss and bits of spiderweb.

A mouse makes a grass nest in the shape of a ball. The mouse hides its nest in tall grass or in a tunnel under the ground.

Careful Builders

Some animals put a lot of work into building their homes. Weaver birds make nests that hang from tree branches. The birds carefully weave grass and leaves together. Weaver birds use their feet and beaks to tie knots in the grass.

 Fun Fact:
The nests of some weaver birds can be so heavy that they break tree branches.

Working Together

Animals can work together to build homes. Termites build **mounds** made out of mud mixed with **saliva**. Other animals cannot easily break through the hard mud.

Polyps are animals that make coral reefs. A polyp builds a **limestone** cup around its body for protection. The cups of the polyps grow together to make a coral reef.

Making a Burrow

Burrows are holes in the ground where some animals live. Gophers use their teeth and paws to dig long, winding tunnels. They make rooms in the deepest parts of the tunnels. The gophers hide their offspring and food in these rooms.

Home Improvement

Some animals live in homes made by other animals. Chickadees use tree holes made by woodpeckers. Chickadees bring grass and moss into the hole. They build a nest for their chicks.

17

Building a Home

Most animals need homes where they can rest and raise their offspring. Homes also keep animals safe from predators. Beavers build lodges. Mice make nests. Gophers dig burrows. How does a polar bear make its **den**?

Amazing But True!

Bald eagles build huge nests high in the tops of trees or cliffs. These nests are called aeries (AIR-eez). Some aeries can be 9 feet (2.7 meters) around and 6 feet (1.8 meters) deep. The nests can weigh 2 tons (1.8 metric tons). Bald eagles add grass and twigs to their nests every year.

Hands On: Build a Nest

Some animals build nests to live in and to raise their young in. Some animals spend a lot of time building their nests. Try this activity and find out if you can make a nest.

What You Need

leaves
bark
dryer lint
blades of grass
string or thread

What You Do

1. Place the leaves, bark, and dryer lint into a nest shape.
2. Weave blades of grass, string, or thread through the nest to hold everything together.
3. While you are building your nest, think of how an animal with no hands does the same task. Does long grass or short grass work better? What trick can you discover to keep everything together? What shape will your nest be?
   Is it easier to make a large nest or a small one?

Glossary

burrow (BUR-oh)—a tunnel or hole in the ground made or used by an animal

den (DEN)—the place where a wild animal lives

limestone (LIME-stohn)—a hard rock made by coral or shells

lodge (LOJ)—a beaver's home; beavers use logs and mud to build lodges in lakes and rivers.

mound (MOUND)—a hill or pile

offspring (OF-spring)—animals born to a set of parents

predator (PRED-uh-tur)—an animal that hunts other animals for food

saliva (suh-LYE-vuh)—the clear liquid in the mouth

survive (sur-VIVE)—to continue to live

Read More

Jango-Cohen, Judith. *Hovering Hummingbirds.* Pull Ahead Books. Minneapolis: Lerner, 2003.

Lynch, Wayne. *Whose House Is This?* Name That Animal! Milwaukee: Gareth Stevens, 2003.

Sullivan, Jody. *Beavers: Big-Toothed Builders.* The Wild World of Animals. Mankato, Minn.: Bridgestone Books, 2003.

Internet Sites

FactHound offers a safe, fun way to find Internet sites related to this book. All of the sites on FactHound have been researched by our staff.

Here's how:
1. Visit *www.facthound.com*
2. Type in this special code **0736825096** for age-appropriate sites. Or enter a search word related to this book for a more general search.
3. Click on the Fetch It button.

FactHound will fetch the best sites for you!

Index